Miracles and Marvels of the Birds and Beasts

Selected and translated by

Fr. Robert Nixon, OSB

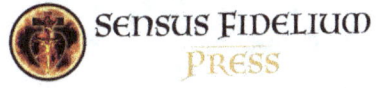
SENSUS FIDELIUM
PRESS

Translated by Fr. Robert Nixon, OSB

ISBN: 978-1-962639-57-6

Book Cover, Book Interior and E-book Design by:
Amit Dey (amitdey2528@gmail.com)

For more information, please visit sensusfideliumpress.com

Contents

◇◇◇◇◇◇◇◇◇◇◇◇◇◇◇◇◇◇◇◇◇◇◇◇◇◇

Translator's Note

According to the book of Genesis, our earliest ancestors, Adam and Eve, first lived in peace with all the animals and enjoyed perfect friendship and harmony with them. But in the course of time, after the wicked serpent tempted Adam and Eve to eat the forbidden fruit, this situation unfortunately ceased to prevail. Although some animals were tamed and domesticated, most of them became afraid of humans, and some even became dangerous to them. Nevertheless, by the grace of God, perfect harmony between human beings and birds and beasts have been witnessed from time to time in miraculous and astonishing ways, especially in the lives of the saints.

Over the centuries, there have been many strange incidents and marvelous happenings involving holy men and women and birds and animals of various kinds. Some of these incidents—such as when a raven saved St. Benedict from consuming poison, or when St. Francis of Assisi befriended a ferocious wolf—are already known to many people, and dearly loved. Yet there are literally hundreds of others, equally wondrous and inspiring, which remain today virtually unknown. It is probably fair to say that very few modern readers will be familiar with the story of Pope St. Leo IX and the remarkable talking dog, or St. Bernard of Clairvaux escaping from werewolves in a forest in France, or St. Pachomius of Egypt who used to ride across rivers on the backs of crocodiles! This collection has deliberately chosen mainly stories which are not well-known, and which mostly cannot be found in any other books in the English language.

The present volume aims at sharing these with young readers, to inspire and entertain them. Many of these stories are taken from a book written in Latin, called Admiranda Orbis Christiani ('Wonders of the Christian World') by Fr. Giovanni Bonifacio Bagatta, which was first published in Venice in 1680. Fr. Bagatta (1649-1702) was a priest in the city of Verona, in Italy. He great work of writing, Admirana Orbis Christiani, was a popular and best-selling book in the 1600s and 1700s. At that time, most people who bought books could still read Latin easily, and Latin was used not only in Masses but also in universities and schools. Some of the stories are taken from the Acta Sanctorum ('Deeds of the Saints'), which is a huge collection of the lives and miracles of a great many saints (about 20,000), which took

almost 300 years to be compiled! The majority
of the stories took place a very long time ago—
some in them happened in the days of the Roman
Empire (which lasted until about 500 or 600), but
most of them took place in the Middle Ages (from
about 500 until 1500). A few of the miracles come
from other ancient sources, too.

These miracles all reflect the awesome and incred-
ible power of God to work through all things in the
universe, including animals. The also often portray
an image of a wonderful harmony and co-opera-
tion between humans and birds, mammals, reptiles
and amphibians. The prophet Isaiah spoke of such
harmony when he made the following prediction:

> *The wolf shall dwell with the lamb, and the
> leopard shall lie down with the kid; and the
> calf and the young lion and the young sheep
> together; and a little child shall lead them. And
> the cow and the bear shall feed; their young
> ones shall lie down together: and the lion shall
> eat straw like the ox. And the baby shall play
> on the hole of the viper, and the small child
> shall put his hand on the cobra's den.*[1]

It is hoped that these short, beautiful and sometimes very strange tales may be the source of

---

[1] Isaiah 11:6-8.

delight and inspiration to readers both young and old, even as they have proven to be for myself,

The humble translator,

Fr. Robert Nixon, OSB
Monk of the Order of St. Benedict,
Abbey of the Most Holy Trinity,
New Norcia, Western Australia

Part One:
Miracles of the Birds

1. Doves

$\diamond$

St. Lucy was an Italian saint during the 300s. She lived in Sicily, an island off the coast of Italy. The pagan authorities at the time tried to force her to renounce her Catholic faith. When she firmly

refused to do so, they tried to burn her to death, but she was unharmed by the flames. They then cut off her head with a sword, and so she died as a martyr for God.

But while St. Lucy was alive, she converted many people to faith in Christ. There was a certain man who lived near her in Sicily, named Geminianus, who very foolishly worshipped idols. In fact, he is said to have had a collection of no less than 30,200 idols in his house! St. Lucy went to see him, to try to convert him from his mistaken belief in the power of these false gods made of stone, wood and metal, and to show him that the real God was the One who reigns in Heaven above.

Now, Geminianus was not very interested at all in what St. Lucy had to say to him. But suddenly, he saw a radiant dove, as white as the purest snow, descend from the Heavens! It stopped above him and made the sign of the cross three times with its wings. He then looked up into the sky and saw a splendid and beautiful vision of the throne of God Himself, shining like fire and gleaming like gold.

Geminianus was astonished by what he saw, and instantly he knew that St. Lucy was speaking the truth to him. Afterwards, he destroyed all his 30,200 idols, and became a faithful believer in the one true God.

✠ ✠ ✠

St. Benedict is one of the most influential saints in the history of the Church. He lived in Italy in the 600s and founded an important order of monks,

who dedicate their lives to prayer, study, simplicity and hospitality to others. St. Benedict had a twin sister called St. Scholastica, who founded many communities of nuns, following the same principles of life as the monks.

The brother and sister, St. Benedict and St. Scholastica, loved each other dearly, and had a close spiritual connection between them. St. Benedict would go and visit her regularly, once each year, and then return home to his own monastery in the evening.

Once, after he visited St. Scholastica, she pleaded with him to stay longer so that they could talk into the night. But St. Benedict said that he could not, as it was against the rules for monks to stay out overnight. But his sister prayed to God that He should send heavy rain, so that her brother would not be able to leave her but would have to stay longer so that they could continue to talk into the night. And God answered her prayer, and a thunderous storm broke out! So St. Benedict remained there that night, and spent the hours of darkness talking with his sister about the wonders of God and the joys of Heaven.

And it happened that just three days afterwards, when St. Benedict had returned to his monastery, he saw a vision of the soul of his beloved sister, St.

Scholastica, ascending into Heaven in the form of a radiant white dove. And, indeed it was found to be the case that St. Scholastica had died at that very instant. St. Benedict ordered her body to be taken to his own monastery at Monte Cassino (not far from Rome), and had her buried there in the same tomb which he had made ready for himself. And he was to pass away too, just forty days later, and was buried beside his sister.

St. Dunstan was an English bishop who lived in the 900s. He was famous for the many miracles which God worked through him. As well as being an outstandingly holy man, he was also a skillful player of the Old English lyre.

It happened that once when he was saying the Mass, when he reached the point where the Holy Spirit is called upon to consecrate the bread and wine, a radiant white dove was clearly seen to descending from Heaven. This beautiful bird continued to hover over the altar as St. Dunstan said the Mass, until it was completed. And then it vanished.

St. Gregory VII was a great pope, who lived during the 1000s. He was a strong leader of the Catholic Church and fought valiantly against its enemies. He was also a wonderful writer, whose words seemed to be always inspired by the Holy Spirit, and filled with all wisdom and insight.

And it happened that whenever St. Gregory sat down at his desk to write something—either a homily, or a letter, or a book—a dove of purest white was seen to appear near him. Sometimes it would hover above him, sometimes it would perch upon his shoulder and seem to be reading the words he was writing, and at other times it would land and walk around his desk. All those who saw this mysterious bird appear were convinced that it was a manifestation of the Holy Spirit, who was there to guide and inspire the holy pope as he wrote.

St. Celestine V was a Italian hermit from the 1200s, who, for most of his life, lived alone and devoted himself entirely to prayer. At times he lived in forests, or on mountains, or in caves, and once even in a swamp. When he grew older a community of men joined him in his life of prayer and good works, and this community grew into a large monastery, on a beautiful mountain in northern Italy called Montagna della Maiella. And when he was very old (over eighty!), he was unexpectedly elected as pope.

Many great signs and wonders appeared at St. Celestine's monastery on Montagna della Maiella. In the early days of the community, when new members first began to be accepted as members, a certain solitary dove of brilliant white plumage would appear in the area. It would always eat from one particular place, where the altar of the monastery church would later be built. And it would walk and fly about among the monks with no fear of them whatsoever, as if it had been raised by them from the nest.

Once the monastery church had been constructed, this dove would frequently enter it even when Mass was being celebrated. And, miraculously, the snowy white bird bowed its head or stood upright or sat down at all the right times during the Mass, just as if it were one of the monks, and understood exactly what was taking place!

2. Eagles

<><><><><><><><><><><><><><><><><><><><><><>

St. Servatius was born in Armenia in the Caucus region, situated between the Middle East and Russia, sometime in the 300s. He ended up being a bishop in Belgium and died in Holland. Traditionally, he is known as one of the 'Ice Saints,'

because his feast day, May 13, is often the coldest day of the year.

It happened that once when St. Servatius was making a journey to Rome to see the pope, he was captured by a band of Goths. These Goths were fierce barbarians, who came from the dark forests of the north of Europe. At that time, they were causing devastation and wreaking havoc throughout Italy.

While being held prisoner by the Goths, an angel appeared to St. Servatius, surrounded by radiant light. This angel took him up and miraculously carried him out of the prison, passing through the walls as if they were mere shadows. The next day, the Goths found St. Servatius to be missing from his dungeon cell, and so went out searching for him. Eventually they found him, sleeping quietly in a field some miles away. And a great eagle sat perched above him, shading him from the sun with one wing and gently fanning him with the other!

In the 200s, when the Roman Empire was still strong, a group of bishops were traveling together to Siponto, a city in southern Italy. They were going to celebrate together the blessing of a new church to St. Michael, the archangel. Amongst these was St. Sabinus, the bishop of Spoleto, in central Italy.

It was summer at the time, and the intense and unremitting heat and blazing sun were afflicting the band of travelers very gravely. So the bishops prayed to God that He should send a refreshing breeze to bring them relief. As soon as this prayer of the holy bishops had been concluded, behold, a splendid eagle of enormous size appeared, and hovered above them! It brought them a two-fold relief, both shading them from the rays of the sun and cooling them with the breezes caused by the flapping of its huge wings.

St. Cuthbert was a monk who became the bishop of Lindisfarne, a town in England, in the 600s. Once when he was traveling southwards, he arrived at the banks of a great river. He spent some time there, both preaching and baptizing the local inhabitants who lived in the area. Now, when the hour of dinner had arrived, an eagle flew down from the sky and alighted on the ground before him. It bore in its talons a large fish, which it graciously placed at the feet of the saint.

And this continued to happen each and every day, so that St. Cuthbert was well provided with food for his travels, in the form of this fish which the eagle would bring to him every day.

In Ireland in the 500s, there was once a troupe of traveling actors and acrobats, who had not been able to find work for some time and were suffering from hunger. So they went to see St. Fintan, the abbot of a local monastery, and requested that the holy man should provide them with some fish to eat; for St. Fintan's monastery was beside a great river. He told them that, unfortunately, he did not have any fish at all to give them, which was indeed quite true.

But one of the acrobats then said to him, "You live here beside a river, and you are a true man of God," he said. "If you simply pray to the Lord, he will certainly provide you with fish, thus supplying both yourself and us with much-needed nourishment!" St. Fintan replied that it was undoubtedly just as easy for God to provide fish as it was for him to provide water or air. So he sent some of his servants to the river to catch a fish. This they did and returned with a huge pike!

However, the pike was of such size, savagery and vigor that no one was able to subdue it. But suddenly, an enormous eagle swooped down from the sky. Grasping the immense fish, it flew up to a great height, and dropped it to the ground. It landed with such force that it was stunned, and easily able to be prepared for eating.

In the marvelous things which are witnessed in the lives of the saints, the glory and compassion of God Himself may be seen. One such amazing thing happened to St. Botolph. St. Botolph was a holy man who lived in England in the 600s and was to become the founder a monastery.

When he was a youth, it happened once that he had been out wandering in the wilderness, as was his custom, carrying with him his book of prayers. But the twilight of evening fell while he was lost in thought, and with it, a violent storm arose. Thus both darkness and rain sorely vexed the young saint. However, the Heavens soon provided Botolph with relief from both. For a brilliant, flaming torch came down from the sky, as if held by some invisible hand, and illuminated the area where the holy youth sat! Next, a huge eagle appeared and hovered above him. With its outstretched wings, the magnificent bird shielded him from the falling rain. And Botolph he was able to spend the night untroubled, reading from his beloved prayer-book.

St. Corbinian was a bishop who lived in France in the 600s. Before he became a bishop, he spent fourteen years as a hermit, dwelling alone in a forest and devoting himself to prayer.

Once, he decided to make a pilgrimage to the distant city of Jerusalem, to visit the land where Christ Himself had lived. He was traveling through the regions of the Turks, accompanied by numerous companions, as well as local Turkish guides and servants. One day, when the hour of dinner had arrived, his Turkish servants brought him a meal, consisting of a dish of red meat—for they had no other form of food available.

However, that particular day was a Friday, when the eating of red meat is not allowed for Catholics. St. Corbinian said nothing as they placed the dish on his table but prayed silently. Then, raising his eyes to Heaven, he saw an eagle flying in the distance. "Look!" he said, "through this bird the merciful Lord shall provide today's meal." And he urged his servants, "Follow that bird!"

This they did, and eventually found the eagle perched on the ground beside a lake. And it held in its talons a magnificent fish—still alive—which it had just captured. The bird flew away, leaving its prey on the ground, as if it were making a gift of it to the pilgrims. And the fish was of such size that it sufficed to provide not only St. Corbinian but all the members of the pilgrimage group with a meal of fish, so that they did not have to eat red meat on a Friday.

𝔗owards the end of the 𝔐iddle 𝔄ges, there was a friar of the Order of Preachers called St. John Vincentinus. The Order of Preachers, also known as the Dominicans, devote themselves to teaching and preaching the Catholic faith.

Now, there was a certain peasant working in the fields, who happened to see an eagle perched near a well. It was a fine bird, with gleaming plumage and piercing eyes. The peasant called out to the bird: "O most noble Eagle, I command you, by the virtues of the holy Friar John, remain where you are; do not fly away from here!" Behold, the bird remained perfectly still! Thus, the peasant was able to approach the eagle easily, and even to take him up in his hands.

The peasant then took the eagle to Friar John and presented it to him as a gift. It was remarkably tame, and became the holy friar's constant companion, sometimes perching on his shoulder, sometimes following him around either walking or flying. St. John Vincentinus used to travel around to villages preaching in those days, and wherever he preached, the eagle would be there, listening to him intently. And whenever his sermons reached their conclusion, the bird would flap its wings vigorously, as if clapping for the preacher and blessing God.

3. Parrots

<<<<<<<<<<<<<<<<<<<<<<<<<<<<<<<<<<<<<<<<<<<<

The noble city of Constantinople was located in the country now called Turkey, but was previously the center of the Eastern Roman Empire, and was sometimes known as "New Rome." In the 800s, Emperor Basil I ruled there, living in a splendid palace in Constantinople. He had two sons—the older one, who was his favorite, was called Prince Constantine, and the younger one was called Prince Leo.

It happened that the older son, Constantine, became ill and died at a young age. His father, Emperor Basil, was overcome with uncontrollable grief. Very unwisely, he employed a certain sorcerer called Santabaren to summon up the ghost of his dead son so that he would be able to see him again. But Prince Leo saw that it was very wrong and misguided for his father to do this, and so he warned him against using the services of the sorcerer Santabaren.

Santabaren was furious about Leo doing this, and so played a cruel trick on the young prince. He hid a dagger in Leo's cloak, and then gave a false warning to Emperor Basil. "Your son, Leo, is planning on killing you!" he said. "If you search his cloak, you will find a dagger hidden there." Basil was fooled by the words of the wizard, and so he did search Leo's cloak. And he found concealed there the dagger, just as Santabaren had predicted!

Although Prince Leo was completely innocent, his father believed that he really had been planning on murdering him. And so he had his unlucky son cast into a dark dungeon, and locked away there. Prince Leo was to spend the next seven years of his life there as a prisoner.

Towards the end of that time, it happened that Emperor Basil was enjoying a splendid banquet in his palace with many guests. He owned a pet parrot, which was in a cage in the banquet hall. And, suddenly, in front of the emperor and all his guests, the parrot exclaimed loudly and clearly, in a voice that seemed to be human: "O Emperor Basil, do not forget your son, Prince Leo, who is at this moment languishing in a dungeon, while you are feasting! Truly I tell you, he is innocent of any crime against you."

Upon hearing these words, the heart of Basil was touched with pity for his son, and he realized that he had imprisoned him wrongly. Immediately, he had Prince Leo released from the dungeon.

Prince Leo was to become emperor himself after this father's death. As well as being a just ruler of his kingdom, he wrote many books on the Christian faith, and was very devoted to the Blessed Virgin Mary. Because of his great intelligence and wisdom, he came to be known as 'Leo the Philosopher' or 'Leo the Wise.' He is venerated as a saint in the Church in the East.

𝕴n 𝔱𝔥e 1000s, the King of Denmark possessed, amongst his many treasures and curiosities, a particularly splendid parrot. This noble and intelligent bird was blessed not only with glorious multicolored feathers, but also with the ability to speak with a voice that seemed to be human. Now, the King of Denmark heard reports of the great holiness and wisdom of St. Leo IX, who was pope at the time. And he resolved to send this fine parrot to the holy pontiff as a gift.

Amazingly, as the bird was being transported, it spontaneously began to say:

> *All you who hear me, know*
> *That to the pope I go;*
> *I'm off to my new home*
> *In great and noble Rome!*

And the parrot continued to repeat these verses as it traveled along its route to Rome.

After it was presented to Pope Leo, a very close friendship at once sprang up between the pope and his new feathered companion. When the bird was first taken into his presence, it is said to have uttered the following verses:

> *O Leo, gracious pope,*
> *In you, the Church does hope!*
> *Most blest am I to meet you,*
> *Rejoicing, do I greet you!*

Furthermore, it is reported that St. Leo, when fatigued or anxious with the demands of his responsibilities as pope, would frequently derive great refreshment and amusement from his conversations with this most talented bird!

4. Ravens and Crows

Blessed Isnard was a Dominican, or member of the Order of Preachers founded by St. Dominic, who lived in the 1200s. He was born in Chiampo, in Italy. From his earliest year, he was extremely devoted to prayer and meditation, and he performed innumerable miracles during his life.

At one time, Blessed Isnard decided to go a live all alone as a hermit in a deserted forest. This was to allow him to contemplate the glory and love of God with all his heart and mind, free from any external distractions. It also permitted him to live a life of great simplicity.

Now it happened that Blessed Isnard become very ill while he was living as hermit. Of course, he had no doctors or medicine in the deserted forest in which he was living, so his situation was very serious. But God had mercy on him, and sent him help, through one of His winged messengers. For as Isnard lay down, shivering with fever and feeling extremely sick and miserable, a raven appeared before him. The glossy, black bird carried in its beak and claws the roots of a certain plant. These it laid before Isnard, bowing its head gently.

Isnard understood that the bird was offering him these roots as a medicine for his illness. He consumed them immediately, and found their flavor to be incredibly sweet and delightful, and he felt as if new strength was beginning to flow through his body. And very soon the holy hermit, Blessed Isnard, was restored to perfect health.

St Paul the Hermit lived in Egypt in the 200s and 300s. He dwelt all alone in a cave for almost one hundred years, and is well-known because another great saint, St. Jerome, wrote his life story.

It is said that for a period of sixty years, every single day, a raven would bring to him half a loaf of bread, and it was by means of this that St. Paul derived his nourishment.

Now, it happened that one day, another saint, St. Anthony the Great, came to visit St. Paul the Hermit. For St. Anthony was eager to learn from St. Paul, and wished to receive some words of wisdom from him. And on the day when St. Anthony was there, the raven brought, not half a loaf of bread, but a whole loaf, so that both saints were able to enjoy a good and satisfying meal.

St. Celestine V was a Italian hermit and monk who lived in the 1200s, and became pope when he was already a very elderly man. We have met the same St. Celestine earlier, with a miracle story of a dove which inhabited the church in his monastery. But this story is about him and a certain crow.

Once it happened that St. Celestine placed a book of spiritual writings which he was reading upon the ledge of his window, so that he could kneel and prayer for a little while. But suddenly, a crow swept down from a nearby tree and snatched it away, carrying it off in its beak. St. Celestine said to the crow, "O Brother Crow, in the name of Our Lord

Jesus Christ, I order you to bring my book back to me!" And at once the crow brought the book back, returning it safely to the window ledge.

St. Columbanus was an Irish monk during the 500s and 600s, who traveled all around Europe converting people to the Catholic faith and foundaing monasteries in many countries. Once, when he was at a monastery in France, he was wearing gloves, for he was working outside and it was very cold. It was time for lunch, so he took off his gloves and left them sitting on a rock outside.

But a certain crow saw these gloves, and swept down and snatched them away. When St. Columbus came out, he spied the crow sitting in a tree, with its gloves lying in its nest. And he spoke thus to the black- feathered bird: "O Crow, you are of that same species of bird which Moses once sent out from the ark, and which failed to return to him! I see now that you have stolen my gloves. Yet I promise you that unless you return these to me without delay, you will never find enough food to feed your chicks!"

Upon hearing these words of warning the crow immediately took up the gloves and returned them to the ground before Columbanus. And not only this, but the bird remained at his feet with his head bowed down, as if sorry for its crime and awaiting its punishment. Upon seeing this, the man of God said to it: "Go forth in peace, Brother Crow, and do not sin again!"

How wondrous is the power of God, the eternal Judge! For He displays His virtues and marvels not only through human beings, but even through the birds of the air!

St. Benedict of Nursia is one of the very greatest saints of the Church. We have already met St. Benedict, in the miracle of the vision of a dove which he saw when his sister, St. Scholastica, died. St. Benedict lived in Italy in the 500s, and founded an Order of monks which was to spread throughout all the world. His life story was written by another

saint, St. Gregory the Great, who was one of the most successful popes in all of history.

After he had founded his first monastery, St. Benedict became very famous because of his holiness and wisdom. But there was a certain priest by the name of Florentius who lived nearby, who became inflamed with jealousy at St. Benedict's reputation for holiness, and this envy soon grew into wicked malice. So one day Florentius took a loaf of bread, soaked it in poison and then took it to St. Benedict, pretending that he wished the saint to bless it for him and to accept it as a gift. St. Benedict took the bread gratefully, but sensing by miraculous insight that it was poisoned, he gave it to a raven which he was in the habit of feeding. And he spoke thus to the bird: "In the name of the Lord Jesus Christ, take this bread to some place where no human shall ever find it or eat it!"

The raven then flew around the bread crowing loudly, as if wishing to obey the saint's instructions but was somehow unable to do so. The man of God then repeated his words: "I say to you, my feathered friend, take this bread and take it far away from here! Then cast it away in some deserted place." Upon hearing this, the raven did exactly as it had been asked. After three days the black-feathered bird returned to the saint, to resume its regular custom of accepting daily a little food from his holy hand.

(We warn our readers that the next miracle is not for the squeamish or faint-hearted. If you are easily frightened or shocked, perhaps skip this one!)

The very first archbishop of the region of Tarantasia in the Alps in France was a certain St. James, who lived in the 400s. Now, even though it is normally cold and snowy in that part of the world, it occasionally becomes very hot in the days of summer. And once when St. James was making a journey, he was almost overcome by the heat of the weather and the sun's fiercely burning rays. So he sought relief under the shade of a large tree, tying up the donkey on which he had been traveling.

But a certain bird, a kind of vicious crow, began to swoop upon the poor donkey. He pecked at the unfortunate creature so fiercely that blood flowed freely from his sides. Moreover, he even snatched one of the donkey's eyes from its socket!

The attendants of the archbishop noticed this gruesome thing, and rushed to tell their master what was happening. So St. James immediately rose from his rest and went to where the donkey stood, and saw the cruel crow still hovering around. He addressed himself to the malicious bird: "O most wicked fowl, who are as black as midnight! I command you in the name of the Lord to restore what you have stolen!"

And immediately, the crow flew away. It returned shortly afterwards, with the donkey's eyeball held in its claw, and gently replaced it into the socket. And the donkey was perfectly well after that, as if nothing had ever happened to it.

5. Geese

St. Werburgh, who lived in the 600s, was the daughter of the King of Sicily, so as well as being a saint she was also a princess. Later in her life, it seems that she traveled to England and founded a convent of nuns there. But it happened that once, when she was still a young woman, she was staying in one of the villages of her father's kingdom. And she learnt that this village was suffering greatly at this time, for a huge flock of wild geese had infested the region and had eaten a large portion of the annual crops.

So St. Werburgh instructed one of her servants to go and call the geese to herself. Naturally enough, the servant thought that this instruction was somewhat foolish, or perhaps a kind of jest; nevertheless, out of pure obedience, he did just as his mistress had instructed (although he expected it to have no effect). Going out to a field where the flock were feeding, he called out to them: "O Geese, come with me to my mistress, Princess Wereburg! For she has ordered me to invite you to her presence."

To the utter astonishment of the servant, the geese appeared to understand him! They assembled themselves into an orderly flock, and walked behind him as he returned to the castle. There St. Werburgh told them, kindly but firmly, that were doing wrong by depriving the local farmers of their crops, and told them that they should depart from that region and trouble them no more. And, behold, that is precisely what happened! To this day, that particular species of wild goose has never again been seen around that village or its surrounding farms.

St. Brigid is one of the patron saints of Ireland, along with St. Patrick and St. Columba. She lived in the 400s and 500s and was the daughter of a Irish chief and a slave, but she was raised by the druids. These druids were a group of mysterious magicians; we do not know much about them, but they are probably most famous now for building Stonehenge in England. But despite being raised by the druids, Brigid became a devout Christian, and eventually founded a monastery at Kildare, in the middle of Ireland.

It is said that one day St. Brigid was out walking when she encounted a flock of geese. Some of these geese were swimming in the water and others flying about, and all honking or quacking noisily. It was then time for prayer, so St. Brigid summoned the birds to herself. Amazingly, they immediately gathered before her, without any fear whatsoever. She then instructed them to be silent for prayer, which they did, seating themselves quietly with great reverence and piety. Once the saint had concluded her prayers, she gave the final blessing and pronounced the customary dismissal, telling then to go forth in peace. And the geese then departed from her to resume their former activities.

St. Rigobert was a an extremely holy monk who lived in the 600s and 700s. He later became bishop of the city of Rheims in the north of France.

Once there was once a certain woman who presented a fine goose as a gift to St. Rigobert. He accepted it with thanks, and handed it to his servant-boy to take care of. But, alas, the goose escaped from the boy's hands, and flew off! The poor boy was deeply dejected and afraid of incurring his master's displeasure and getting into trouble. But Rigobert, far from being angry, looked at the boy with tender compassion. "My son," he said kindly, "do not be saddened over this trivial matter! For the loss of any earthly thing is of but little consequence, as long as we retain the eternal love of God in our

4. San.

S. RIGOBERTUS RHEMENS. ARCHIEP. ORD. S. BEN.

Resbaci ad omnem virtutē occultꝗ recens structo Monͦio Orbacēsi præeſse jube-
tur; poſtea Cathedræ Rbemensi admotꝰ A C. Martello non tantùm multa paſſꝗ
ſed etiā ſede ſuā deturbatꝗ eſt. Tandē Monachi vitā redintegraturꝗ ad ſerā uſꝗ ætatem
rigidiſſimè coegit. Aufert ſæpiꝗ fami ſe āduæ se ultrò offerēti nūꝗ̃ mēse suæ adbibuit.

hearts. Faith, hope and charity are our most valuable treasures, and these can never be stolen away from us or accidently lost! And truly, God has the power to give all things to those who please Him and call upon Him." Upon this, the goose immediately flew back to the boy, and seated itself on the ground before him.

Afterwards, St. Rigobert would never permit this fowl to be killed for the table. Rather, the goose became his constant companion, always walking before him—and apparently even leading the way!—whenever he had to make a journey.

Part Two:
Miracles of the Beasts

1. Bulls, Oxen and Cattle

In the days of the Roman Empire, cruel and bloodthirsty persecutions were sometimes carried out against the followers of Jesus, instigated by the Roman Emperors Nero, Domitian, Diocletian and several others. In those times, they had many horrible and strange methods of torturing and executing people.

One such method was by releasing fierce bulls onto them, normally in a public arena or amphitheatre. Nevertheless, a great many of the histories of these ancient martyrs recount that the bulls who were intended to kill them suddenly became meek and gentle in the presence of the saints, and sometimes lay themselves down at their feet, or even lovingly licked their hands!

St. Martin was a Roman soldier born in Italy in the 300s. After converting to the Christian faith, he resigned from the army and moved to France to become a monk. He was then chosen as bishop of the French city of Tours, and was admired for his holiness, simplicity of life, and wisdom. Today, he is the patron saint of France.

Once it happened that St. Martin was traveling from the city of Trier in Germany, when he encountered a fierce ox upon the way. This particular beast seemed to be controlled by a devil or evil spirit, for it shunned the company of its fellow animals and attacked any humans whom it encountered. It confronted St. Martin with blazing eyes, flared

nostrils and furious bellowings. Just as it was charging at him, the saint commanded it to stand still.

This it did, remaining perfectly immobile before him. St. Martin then commanded the devil to depart from the animal, in the holy name of Christ. After this, the ox completely lost all its savagery. It returned to its herd, and thereafter it exhibited a remarkably gentle and peaceful temperament.

In Ireland in the early Middle Ages, there were many monasteries, where the monks devoted themselves to prayer, to study, and to developing the Christian virtues. One very holy monk was St. Senan, who lived in the 500s.

Miracles and Marvels of the Birds and Beasts

At the monastery where St. Senan lived, it was the custom for the monks of the community each to take turns in looking after the cattle. This was especially needed when the young calves were being separated from the mother cows. For at those times, it was necessary to separate the calves from their mothers for certain periods of time, so that they became used to feeding and looking after themselves.

It happened that St. Senan, who was a mere youth at the time, was a monk at this monastery, and it was his turn to attend to the herd. However, he found that, try as he might, he could not keep the calves from their mothers. While he was separating one calf from its mother, the others would re-unite.

Almost driven to frustration, he took his staff, and drew a line in the ground. After praying sincerely to God, he spoke to the cattle thus: "In the holy name of Christ," said he, "I command you: calves, you stand on this side of the line; and mother cows, you remain on the other side!" And, behold, all the beasts immediately obeyed him! And Senan continued to employ this practice each time it was his turn to keep watch over the herd, and it never failed to work. Thus, he was free to devote his attention to prayer, contemplation and reading, without anxiety or distraction.

When King Veremundo I reigned over the Kingdom of Asturias in Spain in the 700s, he summoned St. Athaulph, who was one of the bishops in his kingdom, to visit him at his royal court. This was in accordance with the established custom of the times, and St. Athaulph was very willingly made the journey to the capital city of the Kingdom of Asturias, Oviedo, to meet the king.

Now the day on which he arrived happened to be Holy Thursday, and he was eager to visit the local church to pray before seeing the king. But some of his associates advised him that the correct protocol was to present himself at the royal court first, before doing anything else. To this, St. Athaulph replied: "It is not so! For surely it is more fitting for me to visit the King of all the Universe, before I call upon a monarch who rules only in a kingdom which is merely earthly!" And thus he betook himself firstly to the cathedral to offer his prayers.

But when King Veremundo heard that Bishop Athaulph had arrived in the city but had not come to see him immediately, he was offended and enraged. He had the bishop arrested and sentenced him to be cast into an arena with a savage bull. But when the bull rushed towards the bishop, it suddenly stopped in its tracks. It ceased from its fury and lowered its head, mooing gently. Then, what is even more remarkable, its horns, which were exceedingly long and sharp, dropped clean off its head!

All present, including the king himself, were filled with wonder and amazement. St. Arnaulph took these magnificent and impressive bull's horns as a memento of this miraculous happening, and they may be seen at the cathedral at Oviedo in Spain to this very day.

And as for King Veremundo, when he saw this miracle, he realized the power of God and repented of his own arrogance. Shortly afterwards, he resigned as king and lived the rest of his life as a monk, devoting himself to prayer and the service of the Lord.

St. Sylvester was born in 1177 in Italy, and lived as a hermit and monk. He performed a great number of miracles, and people flocked to him to request his prayers and advice.

It happened that during the time of St. Sylvester, there was a certain ox that seemed to have become possessed by devils. For, although it had formerly been a tame and gentle creature who had willingly served his master obediently, it had now become totally furious and savage. Its nostrils would flare and its mouth would foam, and it would charge at anyone who approached it. Eventually, its madness exhausted the animal itself, and one day it fell down dead.

News of this came to the ears of St. Sylvester, who was moved by compassion both towards the hapless ox and its unfortunate owner. So he visited the farm, and asked to be taken to the dead ox. And the he spoke to it thus: "Arise, O Brother Ox! Cast off this wicked anger and malice which has taken possession of your heart, and return to your true self— that gentle and obedient animal that your master so loved and valued." And once he concluded this touching speech, the ox came back to life and rose to its feet! Thenceforth, it was again the tame and kindly beast it had formerly been.

St. Francis de Paola was a holy friar, who lived in Italy in the 1400s and became famous for his sanctity and for the many astonishing miracles he worked. Once, when he was in the region of Tortoreto in central Italy, St. Francis heard that a certain local nobleman, the Baron of Cesaro, had a great abundance of oxen on his farm. He knew also that a particular convent in Calabria (also in Italy)

was suffering from an desperate shortage of such animals.

So St. Francis de Paola arranged to see the baron, and humbly requested that he might be generous enough to give some of his oxen to the nuns in Calabria, since he already had too many on his land but the nuns did not have enough. The baron replied that he did indeed have more oxen than he could possibly want or need, but they were all wild and untamed beasts. "You are most welcome to take as many as you like," said the baron to the saint, "that is, if you can manage to capture and restrain them!"

A little later, the nobleman was amazed to see St. Francis leading away a small herd of these wild oxen, who now behaved as gently and submissively as if they had been gentle lambs. What is even more astonishing is that the saint spoke to these animals as if they were intelligent human beings who could comprehend his words, and explained to them that they were needed at a particular convent in Calabria. Then, with no one leading them or showing them the way, the oxen made the journey there, and safely arrived at the convent after just a few days!

2. Dogs

<<<<<<<<<<<<<<<<<<<<<<<<<<<<<

During the time when the twelve apostles of Christ were still alive, they had many enemies, who tried to silence, suppress or even kill them. One such enemy was Simon Magus, or Simon the Sorcerer. We read in the Acts of the Apostles how he once tried to obtain the miraculous powers of the Holy Spirit which the apostles possessed for himself, by offering to pay them a sum of money.[2]

Sometime after Christ had died, risen from the dead and ascended into Heaven, both St. Peter and Simon Magus were living in Rome, which was regarded as the capital city of the civilized world in those days. St. Peter was preaching the true message of Jesus, but Simon Magus was preaching a false version of the Gospel, which he had made up himself. So Simon Magus became an enemy of St. Peter, and was very jealous of him.

And once this wicked sorcerer and false apostle, Simon Magus, tied a fierce dog to the gates of the house of a certain citizen of Rome, called Marcellus. He did this because he knew that St. Peter—whom

---

[2]See Acts 8:9-24.

he considered to be a rival to his own magical arts—frequently visited Marcellus, and he was hoping that the dog would attack St. Peter. But when St. Peter arrived, the dog greeted him with gentle friendliness. The apostle then released the dog from his leash. But, alas, for Simon Magus! For the hound then turned upon him, ripping his fine and showy vestments to shreds.

St. Patrick is well-known as the patron saint of Ireland, and St. Patrick's Day is celebrated with great joy today all around the world. St. Patrick himself lived back in the 400s. He was born in Britain but journeyed across the sea to Ireland to preach the Gospel to the people who lived in that green and pleasant land.

In the days when St. Patrick was doing this important missionary work, King Leogarius ruled over Ireland as its main monarch. Now King Leogarius soon became concerned that St. Patrick's preaching would undermine his own power and authority and encourage the people to rebel against him. So, he arranged for a savage hunting dog to be set upon St. Patrick, a great, black mastiff hound. And this was done in accordance with his orders.

But as the huge beast rushed towards St. Patrick, he looked at it directly in the eye, without the slightest trace of fear. At once, the dog was rendered completely motionless. And it remained perfectly still and immobile, as if it were made from stone! And this dog-shaped stone (or rather, the dog that was turned into a stone by St. Patrick) may still be seen in Ireland to this very day.

In the 500s or 600s, somewhere in France, a certain man, Attila by name, was out hunting with his pack of hounds, who were pursuing a large boar (or wild pig.) The boar, terrified of the barking pack of fierce dogs, took refuge in a nearby dense forest. Now in that forest their lived at the time a certain holy hermit named St. Basolus, who was following a life of prayer, simplicity and solitude, alone among the woods.

Once in the forest, the boar rushed to St. Basolus and lay down at his feet, as if seeking protection from him. The snarling dogs which were pursuing it soon arrived. But upon seeing the saint, their ferocity instantly vanished, and they became as gentle as lambs! The pack of hunting hounds left the woods quietly, leaving the boar unharmed in the care of the hermit.

And from that day onwards, it was found that if any animal ever sought refuge in those particular woods, no hunting dogs would ever dare to pursue it there.

We have already met St. Martin in a story about an ox that was possessed by a devil, and which he cured. He was the bishop of the city of Tours in France in the 400s and is the patron saint of France.

It happened that once St. Martin was making a tour of his diocese on foot, together with a group of his clergy. As they passed through the green meadows of the countryside, by chance, they encountered a hunting party who were pursuing a rabbit. Now the unfortunate rabbit found itself surrounded by the hunter's pack of dogs in the middle of an open field. This field had no trees or bushes, and so there was no hiding place for the poor rabbit. So it seemed to have no chance at all of escaping from the fleet-footed canines.

Overcome with fear, the rabbit crouched to the ground, quivering with terror. But the kind heart of St. Martin was filled with compassion for the poor animal's plight. He addressed the dogs, ordering them, in the name of Jesus, to spare the life of the defenseless rabbit. Amazingly, the pack of dogs at once became perfectly still, as if they were affixed to the ground where they stood. And the rabbit fled away to safety.

St. Roch was a friar of the Order of St. Francis, who lived in the 1300s. He was very dedicated to serving those suffering from the plague, also known as the 'bubonic plague' or the 'black death', which is believed to have killed a third of the population of Europe during the Middle Ages. Because of his dedication to helping people infected with the plague, St. Roch is frequently prayed to for protection against plague and other

contagious diseases. He is also the patron saint of dogs, for reasons which are revealed in the following miracle story.

It happened that while St. Roch was looking after poor people who were suffering from the plague, he himself became infected with the same dreaded disease. He took refuge in an isolated forest, to prevent spreading the fatal plague germs to anyone else and remained there in solitude for some time.

Now there was a certain rich nobleman by the name of Gothard, who had a castle near the forest where St. Roch was living. This Gothard was a keen hunter and had a fine pack of hunting hounds. One day as he sat at his table, one of his hounds leapt up and snatched a piece of meat from his hand, and quickly carried it off. Gothard was surprised and perplexed, for his animals were extremely well-trained and normally well-behaved. He asked his servants about it, but they could offer him no explanation.

The next day, the same thing happened again and again the day after. So Gothard, filled with curiosity, resolved to follow the dog if he again snatched his food from his hand. And the very next day, the dog did again snatch some food from his master's hand, and then hurried off!

But this time, Gothard followed him. And he found that the dog entered the nearby woods. The hound took the piece of meat to a small hut, and presented it to the dweller of the hut—who was none other than St. Roch! He then realized that (spurred on by the Holy Spirit) the dog had been taking a little food to the forest each day, to provide nourishment for the saint. St. Roch accepted the morsel with gratitude and gave the dog his blessing.

Once the abbot (or superior) of a particular monastery somewhere in Europe had cause to send one of his monks on an errand to another monastery, located a great distance away. But the monk told the abbot that, unfortunately, he had never been there before and did not know the way. So the abbot turned to his dog, and said to the animal: "My friend, please show this brother the way to the monastery to which I am sending him!"

And the dog, apparently hearing the words of his master clearly and understanding them with perfect comprehension, led the monk to the requested destination without hesitation.

In one of our earlier stories, we encountered St. Leo IX and his remarkable feathered friend—a parrot, who could hold intelligent conversations as if it were a human. St. Leo IX was a pope during the 1000s, and a wise and holy ruler of the Catholic Church. As well as the miraculous talking parrot, there are several other amazing incidents and events in his life. We will hear about one such miracle now.

During the time that St. Leo was pope, a dog was discovered who spoke with a human voice. Instead of barking, it would exclaim: "Deus meus!" (that is, "My God!", in Latin). The fame of this wonder spread very widely, and it attracted a great number of pilgrims, who were eager to see and hear the amazing talking dog. St. Leo himself went and witnessed it himself. He confirmed the truth of the miracle and bestowed his apostolic blessing on all those present.

It is also said that shortly after St. Leo was elected as pope, a miracle was witnessed to happen through a humble rooster. For at the break of dawn, instead of crowing in the customary way, the rooster would sing forth: "Papa Leo!" ("Pope Leo!"). Many citizens of Rome heard this and were able to attest to the truth of this wonder.

St. Bruno, like St. Leo IX, lived in the 1000s. He was the founder of the Order of Carthusian monks. These monks live a life of great silence, solitude and simplicity of life, and are often regarded as the

strictest religious order in the Catholic Church. In Carthusian monasteries, the monks wake up in the middle of the night, and go to prayer in the chapel, beginning at 12:15am. This prayer can then last for two hours!

Before founding his monastery, St. Bruno lived for a time as a hermit in an isolated wilderness region, in the Italian province of Calabria. Once the count of that province, Count Roger, was out hunting with his pack of hounds. Now these were all very savage dogs, trained to hunt bears, wolves and wild boars.

It happened that this fearsome pack came across St. Bruno. At once they stopped their snarling and growling, and all became perfectly silent. And they stood still before the saint with their heads lowered, as if in respectful veneration of him. This event was witnessed by Count Roger himself, who testified to many people about this wonderful and strange miracle.

3. Bears

It is recorded that in the early days of the Church, when Christians were being persecuted and killed by the Roman Empire, many were sentenced to death by having ferocious beasts released upon them. This was normally done in a public arena, where onlookers could witness the bloodthirsty and gruesome spectacle of people being killed by wild animals. And among the animals which were used for this purpose were bears.

But it very often happened that when the fierce bear came into the presence of the faithful Christian whom it was supposed to kill, it did not attack them at all, but became instantly tame and gentle. This happened with St. Cerbonius, the bishop of Populonia in Italy. The bear that was sent in to kill him instead gently embraced him and began to lick him affectionately. With St. Domitilla, who was a niece of the emperor Domitian who became a follower of Christ, much the same thing happened. With St. Pontius, a bishop, the bear that was supposed to kill him sat down at his feet, and played as if it were his pet.

And this miraculous phenomenon—of bears suddenly becoming tame and gentle—was seen to happen with a great many early Christians who were sentenced to death for their faith.

Marcus Aurelius was emperor of the Roman Empire about 150 years after the birth of Christ. He was a very intelligent man, being an accomplished scholar and philosopher as well as a ruler, and he wrote some excellent books which are still read today. But despite this, he was also a cruel persecutor of the early Christians. During the time when Marcus Aurelius was reigning as emperor, a certain young maiden, St. Columba, had been arrested because of her Christian faith.[3]

St. Columba was sentenced to public humiliation. This was a form of punishment in which the condemned person was placed in some public place, such as a town square, and all passers-by and onlookers were then invited to mock them and insult them.

Now, most of the onlookers and passers-by did not make fun of St. Columba at all, for they sensed that she was more worthy of their respect and

_____
[3]This is not the same St. Columba who is one of the patron saints of Ireland.

admiration than of their mockery and they knew that she was a noblewoman of high birth, who had committed no crime deserving punishment.

But a certain young man, Barueham, was there. He was a particularly rough, rude and stupid fellow, and full of arrogance and malice. So he started to insult St. Columba and make fun of her.

Just then, suddenly a huge bear appeared in the square, as if from nowhere! Without hesitation, it struck Barueham to the ground with its massive paws. It then stood over him, as he lay flat on the ground and utterly terrified. The bear looked intently at St. Columba, as if it were asking her: "O blessed Columba, what do you wish me to do with this wretch? Should I kill him, or tear his arms off, or snap his legs? Or should I let him go?"

St. Columba, being merciful and compassionate, then spoke to the bear: "Let him go, my friend! For Christ has commanded us to forgive those who insult us, and to treat even our enemies with charity." So the huge, lumbering bear at once stood back, and let Barueham scurry off to safety. Needless to say, the youth, who had been arrogant and outspoken just a few minutes before, was now pallid with fear and trembled like a leaf.

The whole crowd of onlookers were astonished at this marvel. And it was soon reported to the ears of the emperor, Marcus Aurelian. Frustrated that his plans to humiliate St. Columba had been thwarted, he ordered a great bonfire to be built and set alight, encircling both St. Columba and the bear. It was his plan now that both of them should be burnt to death.

This was done, but the bear easily escaped the blaze by nimbly climbing a nearby wall. But the fierce flames of the fire were quickly closing in on poor St. Columba!

However, just before they reached her, dark clouds suddenly formed in the sky. And rain poured down, extinguishing the fire and thus saving the life of this brave young saint.

There was in Italy, sometime in the last days of the Roman Empire, a certain holy hermit, called St. Florentius. He lived in a small hut in the country-side and survived by looking after sheep. St. Florentius himself would devote himself entirely to prayer, the study of Scriptures, and meditation on the glory of God. But he had a young servant who led his small flock of sheep out to pasture each day.

Now it happened that, one day, this servant went missing! What exactly happened to him, no-one knows. Perhaps he decided to return to civilization to seek his fortune elsewhere, or perhaps he was abducted by bandits, or perhaps some fierce beast of the forest had captured him. Regardless of the unknown fate of the missing servant, St. Florentius was left without anyone to help him take care of his flock of sheep.

So the saint went into a nearby forest. Now a huge bear dwelt within that forest, and soon St. Florentius came face to face with the savage creature. Looking it boldly in the eye, he said: "O Sir Bear, I have need of your services! For I have no-one to pasture my sheep. Perhaps you would help me to do this, please?"

And—wonder of wonders—the bear nodded its head as if in agreement with the request of the holy hermit. It obediently followed St. Florentius out of the forest. From that day forth, it lived in St. Florentius's hut with him, and each day it would lead his small flock of sheep out to pasture.

St. Marinus lived in the 300s in Italy. He was a skilled worker in stone and built for himself a small stone chapel in a remote region on the eastern side of Italy. He lived in this chapel as a hermit, dedicating his life to offering prayer and praise to God in solitude and simplicity of life. After he died, a village grew up around this chapel, which became a place of pilgrimage. In time, it became a town. Today, it is the location of the tiny Republic of San Marino—one of the very smallest independent nations in the world.

St. Marinus owned a faithful donkey, which he rode upon whenever he needed to make a journey. But it happened that once when the saint was riding along on his donkey, a bear leapt out

at him. St. Marinus was thrown off the back of the donkey, and the bear attacked it ferociously, killing it.

St. Marinus then stared hard at the bear. The bear looked back at him guiltily and seemed to realize that it had committed a great crime in killing the saint's donkey. Then the bear knelt, as if offering its own back to St. Marinus. He then mounted it and rode upon it, exactly as if it were a donkey or horse! And this bear continued to serve St. Marinus in place of his donkey for many years to come to the great astonishment of all who witnessed this strange thing.

4. Wolves

◇◇◇◇◇◇◇◇◇◇◇◇◇◇◇◇◇◇◇◇◇◇◇◇◇◇◇◇◇◇

St. Eusorgius was the bishop of the Italian city of Milan in the 300s, back in the days when the Roman Empire was still in existence. He was inspired by God to undertake a very strange and arduous but noble quest—to travel to the East and find the remains of the three wise kings who had visited Christ when He was an infant, and to take their bodies back to bury them respectfully at his own cathedral in Milan.

So, St. Eusorgius set out with a sturdy wagon led by two powerful oxen. For many weeks he journeyed, eventually arriving at the great city of Constantinople (located in modern day Turkey, but at that time the capital of the Byzantine Empire). There he discovered the resting place of the bodies of the three wise kings—Melchior, Caspar and Balthazar—and placed these reverently upon his wagon to take them back to Milan.

But as he was traveling carrying this precious cargo, while going through a deserted wilderness, suddenly an enormous wolf attacked the oxen which drew the wagon. With snarling jaws, razor-sharp teeth, and blazing eyes, it soon killed both of the beasts, literally tearing them to pieces!

St. Eusorgius was not only appalled to witness this bloodthirsty and gruesome slaughter of these innocent oxen before his eyes, but he also knew that, without them, there was no way he could move the heavy wagon. So he firmly commanded the wolf to take the place of the oxen.

Instantly its ferocity came to an end, and the giant wolf lowered its strong shoulders to accept the yoke which the oxen had formerly carried, and pulled the wagon all the way back to Italy! And to this day, many people believe that the bodies of the three wise King from the East who visited the baby Jesus—Melchior, Caspar and Balthazar—are to be found in the ancient Basilica of St. Eusorgius in Milan.

The monastery at Cluny in France was founded in 909, and became one of the largest and most influential monasteries in Europe for several centuries. Many of the abbots of the community of monks who lived there became saints. The second abbot of Cluny Abbey was St. Odo, who lived during the 900s.

St. Odo liked to make pilgrimages to the tombs of saints, and once he was traveling to Tours, to visit the tomb of St. Martin. It was a very dark and moonless night, and he was making his way through a deserted swamp. And it happened that the area was infested with foxes. These animals would strike at him out of the darkness, and he suffered from innumerable bites from their small but very sharp teeth. Eventually a great number of foxes encircled him. Now foxes are normally afraid of humans, but these were particularly vicious and hungry ones, and the fact that there were so many of them made them bold enough to launch an attack on a human being.

Just as St. Odo was looking with dread at the beady eyes of this pack of foxes glowing in the darkness, suddenly a great wolf leapt out! It was of immense size, and immediately all the foxes ran away, terrified. Next, the wolf looked upon St. Odo with its brave and loyal eyes and made a gesture with its head for him to follow. It then led the saint to safety, protecting him from any further attacks or perils until he reached his destination.

St. Bernard was a monk who lived in the 1100s. He was the abbot of a very holy monastery at Clairvaux, which is a beautiful valley in France. St. Bernard's wisdom and sanctity was so outstanding that he was often called upon to resolve disputes, both within the Church and between kings, princes and other members of the nobility.

Once St Bernard was traveling through Burgundy, to negotiate peace between the Count of Forens and the Count of Vienna, who were at war with each other at the time. Passing through a certain village, he was told about two ferocious beasts, known in the local language as 'werewolves,'[4] who inhabited a nearby forest. The monks who accompanied him urged him to go by a different rout, but St. Bernard refused to change his planned course, and so they continued by the forest.

Now the two beasts suddenly rushed out at them, with terrible growling and foul breath, as if to devour them. The monks huddled around Bernard in fear, and cried out "Holy Father, save us!" Bernard said, "Why do you fear, you men of little faith?" He made the sign of the cross, and instantly

---

[4]The word given in the original Latin text (as a word taken from the local language) is 'varol,' which seems to be a form of the Old French word 'garuol,' meaning a werewolf. There were many legends in circulation featuring werewolves in France at this time, but (since werewolves are purely imaginary animals) it seems certain that they were just regular wolves who had developed a taste for human flesh. In most of the Medieval legends, the creatures described as 'werewolves' do not actually transform into human beings at all.

the two werewolves were paralyzed, and rendered as motionless as stone!

St. Francis of Assisi is one of the most famous and dearly loved of all the saints in the Catholic Church. He was born into a rich and noble family in the town of Assisi in Italy in the 1200s. When he was a young man, he gave up all his wealth and position to live a life of simplicity and self-denial for the love of Christ and for the service of the Church.

Now in those day, there were many wolves in Italy. One of them in particular was terrorizing the town of Gubbio. This bloodthirsty and ravenous beast captured and devoured not only sheep and cattle, but even the small children of the townspeople.

St. Francis had pity on the plight of these people, and so bravely went out himself, all alone and with no weapons, to confront the dreaded wolf. "O Brother Wolf," he said when he had come face to face with the creature, "you are terrifying the good people of Gubbio, and wreaking death and destruction across the land! But if you stop these wicked actions, I promise you that the citizens of Gubbio will henceforth provide you with sufficient food so that you will not go hungry."

Upon hearing these words, the wolf seemed to understand them perfectly. It nodded its great hairy head gently, and meekly followed St. Francis back to the town, as if it were a tame lamb. And afterwards, the people of Gubbio would offer the animal a little food each day. The formerly ferocious wolf would wander around the town like a peaceful and friendly dog and became like a beloved pet to all the people who lived there.

5. Frogs, Toads and Crocodiles

St. Benno was bishop of the city of Meissen in German, in the 1000s. When he had some free time from his duties as a bishop, it was his custom to take walks by himself through the fields, praying and meditating. Once it happened that he came by a swamp and found the croaking of the frogs to be so loud and insistent that he was not able to pray.

So, he commanded the frogs to keep silence which they immediately did. But a little while later, he thought of the canticle in the book of Daniel in the Old Testament, which says: "All you who move in the waters, bless the Lord! Bless of you the Lord, all creatures of the Lord!"[5]

Reflecting to himself that the chorus of the frogs croaking was perhaps more pleasing to their Creator than their silence, and perhaps even more pleasing than his own prayer, he implored the frogs to resume their former song in praise of God. And

---

[5] See Daniel 3:79.

immediately the Heavens and the fields were once again filled with the sound of their loud croaking!

We have encountered already St. Leo IX, who served as pope in the 1100s, and we have read about his amazing miracles involving talking parrots, talking dogs, and talking roosters. The following miracle does not involve any talking animals, but it does feature a particularly vicious and venomous toad.

It is related that when Pope St. Leo IX was still a small boy, as he lay sleeping in his bed one night in his family's castle, he awoke to find a great toad sitting on his chest. This toad was of a poisonous species which inhabited the region. In panic, he grasped at the animal, which then leapt on to his face, and spat its venom onto his cheeks.

Little St. Leo gave out such a cry of agitation that the whole household came to where the boy slept. The chamber was searched thoroughly, but not a trace of the toad was to be found anywhere.

For some time afterwards, Leo suffered greatly, for the toad's terrible venom had been absorbed into his skin. His face, throat and chest became horribly swollen, and he was confined to bed for some two months. Indeed, the doctors had all begun to despair of his life, and to believe that he would surely die very soon.

Yet one night, St. Leo had a dream in which he saw a holy and kindly old man, with a long beard of the whiteness of snow and clad in a robe of glowing radiance. This man was descending to him from a staircase which seemed to come from Heaven itself. He held a cross in his right hand, with which touched St. Leo's mouth. And instantly he felt better!

He then asked the man who he was. To this the old man replied, "I am St. Benedict, the founder of monasteries and the father of monks!" When Leo had awoken, he was found to be completely cured of his illness. And thereafter, he always had a particular affection for the monks of the Order of St. Benedict; and, after he had been elected pope, he tried to support and encourage Benedictine monasteries as best as he could.

We have already heard of miracles involving St. Celestine V, who was a pope in 1200s, and doves and ravens. But long before he was elected as pope, when he was still a youth, he spent many years as a hermit.

Once, when he was still a young man and a hermit, St. Celestine lived a solitary life in a swampy area, which was infested with thousands of venomous toads, salamanders and serpents. But his mind was so deeply fixed on the contemplation of the glory of God, that he hardly noticed these creatures at all. Indeed, while he was sleeping, they would often crawl over him and even settle upon him! Yet they caused him neither the slightest disturbance nor harm.

St. Pachomius was a monk who lived in the deserts of Egypt in the 300s. The virtue of St.

Pachomius was so great that he was able to tread upon serpents and scorpions without suffering any harm. And this wondrous grace of friendship with animals extended even to crocodiles. For whenever he needed to cross a river, he would summon a crocodile— of which there are many of in the Nile and other rivers of Egypt. The crocodiles would then calmly permit him to stand upon their backs and would carry him safely over the waters to the other side of the river!